BREAK

A SELF-HEALING JOURNEY

CHRISTINE MARIE

for those who believed in me
when i could not believe in myself

you know who you are

contents

when i was a little girl, i carried the ancestral traumas of my mother and father in my own body. frozen, i stood pressed up against the barren white wall, helplessly watching as they would be taken under by forces bigger than they could comprehend— bigger than anything i, myself, could comprehend. as a child who felt extremely sensitive and empathetic, i crumbled underneath the weight of every unspoken piece of turmoil.

instead of voicing my emotions, i shriveled inside my own skin and the expressions of self were little to none. not wanting to be an extra burden on my already dysfunctional family, i shrunk myself down to a size that was invisible. all the while, i drowned inside the shadows of both my mother and father and completely lost sense of who i was. their stories attached to me as if they were my own. it was as if i had stolen my own identity. i've been trying to find my way back ever since.

so whenever i could, i began to form words onto paper, expressing all of which i kept in for years. the more i allowed spirit to flow through me, the less internal heaviness i felt. not only had i begun coming home to the little girl i once abandoned, but i started to discover the woman i was meant to become.

throughout my young adolescent years, my own
struggle with mental health hit rock bottom and
the truth of my existence came crashing down
on me. i didn't know it then, but this rock bottom
transformed into an awakening i could have never
predicted. i discovered the only way out of the
darkness was through it.

it was within that hollow space of emptiness where
i uncovered my own story and true divinity. while
being forced to face all i tried to bury and leave
behind, i unearthed the biggest disconnection of
all—the relationship between myself and my own
mind. body. and soul.

this collection of poetry is not only a journey of
healing and self-discovery, but it also serves as a
connection back to the little girl who was once so
afraid to be heard, loved, and seen. i dedicate this to
her and to anyone out there who has never had the
chance to fully express their truth.

my hope is that by exposing the marrow of my
bones, it gives others the courage to do the same.

quiet
the
mind

i have always kept in
a collection of stories
worth telling
but never felt
worthy of their meaning
my lips tightly sewn shut
prevents others from opening theirs
but by remaining silent
i sacrifice all of me
and if i disappear
who will be the spine that holds
all of these scattered pages
that i am made out of
together

we all battle wars
inside our own heads
yet the stigma around perfection
disables our voices
from speaking out about the constant fight
against the triggering crossfires
we seldom make peace with
but the bullets come in quick
carving holes inside my skin
i stand still and strong
holding up my mighty head
as if nothing were wrong
yet here i am,
gasping for my last breath
fallen and blood spoiled
as i find my feet buried
in the narrowing trenches
in the middle of the battlefield

i cannot move
i do not know how to

so tell me when will it end
when will i begin to
wave the white flag
and bear witness to
the no-man's-land

the front lines of our minds

the highs are high
the lows are low

there is no such thing as in-between

i wonder
if my mother
could have seen
her own worth
if she would have painted
the sickness
out of her head
and turned it into
creative medicine

mental illness
are two words
that invite her to dance
they spin her clarity around
into a clouded mess

when everybody else
continues to suffer
she suffers
a silent death

i feel her pain as if it were my own

please do not write me
another worthless prescription
self-love cannot
be bought
nor fixed
with external medicine

i am afraid
there will never be
a way out
of this darkness
so long as i
keep chasing it

these twisted thoughts
create a desolate garden
inside my head

i try to shrink them small

but they possess roots
far too restless
and deep

i cannot imagine
a life without
their hold

but i am thinking

i would like to
someday
untangle them

on my own

if only my father was aware
of the genuine kindness
pouring out of his bones
then maybe he could
break free
from the need to
sabotage his veins
in order to feel the love
he so inherently
deserves

generations of self-abuse

winter in detroit
is coming
time is lost
and so is my head
weighing heavy
on these shoulders
i cannot make it through
another frozen night
without you here
next to me

go ahead
snow-covered sheets
smother me

i know
i cannot save you
i know
i have no control
in the way your story ends

but my hands are here
reaching out
for you
hoping that somehow
someday
yours will grasp them
and follow
me home

awake at night
she suffers silently
waiting for someone
for anyone
to save her
from her own
self-destruction

sometimes
you wake up
next to the morning sun
with fire fueling your soul
only to fall into bed
the same exact day
feeling emptier than before

christine marie

quiet
the voices
inside your head

she said

they are only as loud
as you make
them out
to be

there is realness in pain
there is darkness
there is shame
dangling at the ends
of our toes
some say *it gets better*
tell me when it does
until then i sit and linger
in a sea full of
pangs and throes

what if this place
that we are all living in
is nothing
but a dream
where we choose to live
fully awake
or dead asleep

we are more than sheep
we are spiritual beings

i was like a child
when i found you
you gave me offerings
as sweet as sugar
i was instantly addicted

i am always drowning
further into you
your current strong
pulling me near the inner surface
of your waves
and if gasping for air
is what saves me
then i would rather die knowing
i was deep inside
the one thing
that made me feel
the most alive

my heart has a tendency to grow
as big as the sea
some days i wish it were
only made of sand

i want to become
every single moving particle
traveling within you

i could have loved you for the rest of my life
i could have loved you beyond the phases of
infinite moons

i do not have to assume
love makes you blind
as soon as i fell for you
i could no longer
see my way out

no one ever told me—
no one ever told me
waking up
with swollen eyelids
and soaked pillowcases
wasn't love

shame hides beneath
the white threads of my bedsheets
covers me in smoke signals
waiting to dream
my black stained pillowcase
knows all my secrets
it knows both my name
and yours
as i sleep
i hope to whisper
the sound of your voice
right out of me

i only realized
how empty i felt
when waking up
next to you
and waking up
without you
killed me both
the same

there is nothing quite as nostalgic
as november rain

what if
the only thing
you have ever known
about love
is that it's fleeting

tell me
how do you ever come back
from that abandoned feeling

once he left
her heart exploded
for the very first time

she was not as afraid of losing him
as she was afraid to discover
the person she had become
while she was with him

ignorance is not bliss

breaking free

i ran to
the city of dreams
to erase you
from my own

new york, new york

christine marie

i thought *leaving* meant *leaving you behind*

i force myself not to think of you
when all i want
is to run into
your empty arms

christine marie

i cannot see the light at the end
though i feel its rays
reflect off every pore
on my beaten face
i do not know
the fool that i've become
following the footsteps
of a ghost
who does not live here

anymore

i wonder if i will see you
in another lifetime
or will i be forced to spend
the long days ahead
forgetting your name

all over again

it does not matter
how many letters you write
you will always find more words to say
to the one that got away

we cling to every word
every single piece
that makes our hearts
twist and turn
the madness
the fear
we cannot
will not
do not
let them go

my dear
let them go

i turn my pain
into poetry
in hopes to write
the toxic love
i have for you
out of me

i hate the way
you made me believe
loving you
was better than
loving myself

did seeing me
for the first time in months
remind you of
somebody you used to know

i wonder if it is possible
to force someone so far out of your head
that the strands of that person
are stripped away
that their imprint in your blood
is fully erased
pulling the thoughts they are tangled to
right out of your veins

must you completely rip apart
the memory of the love
as well as
the memory of the abuse
at the very same time

is this what you must do
in order to survive

i tried to make a home
out of a monster
but all i did was
suffocate my interior
i did not know how fragile i was
until all the walls came
crumbling down
and i was left
to dust off
to pick up
the fractured pieces
of what was left of us

she found the same ecstasy
in losing you

as she did
in loving you

truth be told
i never thought i would make it through
most of those december nights

your hands follow
up and down my spine
like a river that runs
through a land of forest pines
just like the weight on my back
i carry you with me
wherever i go

living within a world of permanence
veils a lack of personal freedom
so i plunge my spirit
into altering horizons
and flow along the rapid currents
constantly changing direction
without attaching to people
i know will someday
leave me

fear of abandonment

you cannot understand
the mess behind your own chaos
until you breathe in
fresher air

tell me
where does your heart go
when your mind wanders
far away from your soul

your inability
to love
who i am
will not define
who i will
become

where is my faith
when i need it the most
expectations are the enemy
caught in between
what i know
and what i've fought so hard to bury

what is the point in new beginnings
when i have not let go
of tired endings

sometimes i fear
i need more than
what this world
has to offer

the confusion
of my everyday reality
continues to
deplete me
even when i find the strength to stand
the sense of not belonging
rattles the fragility
of my spine
pulling the earth
right out from
underneath my feet

saying the words
i am depressed
flutters holes inside my stomach
opening up a gateway to a distant past
i long to forget
but i remember
of course i do
i tell others
do not be ashamed—
you are not your mental illness
yet, i still find myself
curled up on the bathroom floor
holding my womb
shaken down
worried as hell
that i'll return back to rock bottom
and scream loud enough
for the entire world to hear
when i am desperate in despair

end the stigma

you are not
your *disease or diagnosis*

my dear
you *are so much more*

you are a transmutation of divine alchemy
misunderstood by a broken society

if i fear
the judgment of others
i may never find a safe space
to spread my wings

the cost of sharing our vulnerabilities
comes at the price
of detaching from our egos

no matter how fragile
nobody
not even a stranger
mirrors the destruction
of the tiny
fragmented pieces
we are composed of
quite like we do
ourselves

i thought you saw the spark inside of me
until your words painted a picture of envy
the pain lingered until i decided
i cannot grow in alignment
with the woman i was born to be
if i continue to live my life
pleasing someone who is incapable of
fully seeing me

i will not change who i am
to appease your insecurity

my dearest friend
i never wanted
to cause you
any pain
i only wished to
take it all away

unapologetically
show up in this world
be who you truly are
those that fully see you
will not disrupt your growth
they will only encourage it more

i knew i could not fully accept her
for who she was in all her imperfections
until i began to accept myself
in all of mine

people will learn
how to treat you
by the way
you treat yourself

i cannot
i will not
apologize
for the way you confuse
me following my dreams
being the same
as leaving you
behind

our greatest battles are often drawn
not between one another
but with the resistance we meet
the moment we start leaning into
our truest selves

she blamed her failures
on all of those
who did not
believe in her
when all it took
was her finally
believing in herself

i am uncertain
if i am afraid of the world
hearing my truth
so much as i am afraid of
listening to it myself

not only do we owe it
to ourselves
but we owe it
to the world
to muster up all courage
and bravely speak up
when no one else will

fear is a looming cloud
its mystery, my perverse inhibitory
hindering me from a warrioress victory
and every embrace of sullen sky
spirals into prolonging apathy
but then when it passes
because it always does
a yearn for a dim oblivion returns
tracing a lack of stability
defining my attachment
to chaos
and uncertainty

self-sabotage

what is the point in all of this
i've numbed until i felt nothing
covered up in shame
i'd rather stay cold and hungry
than to give my voice a stage
for fear my whole body would unravel
and i would become unglued
by a handful of grace

so here i am—
granting myself the opportunity
to pour out poetry
like it is the morphine drip
soothing my agony
like it is the oxygen mask
keeping me alive
i might as well be buried
without my lifeline

loneliness
threw me out
into the earth
i followed the wind's harmonies
and every muddy puddle of rain
through a brush of velvet trees
where whispers echo
a long-lost friend
inside the valley
i am cradled in

a quest to the pacific northwest

we begin moving forward
on our journey ahead
once we lay old ghosts
to rest

the road to self-discovery
is one
that never ends

Mother Earth disconnects
the power of madness
inside of me

a life without meaning
to me
is not a life worth living

i would die
a thousand times
to find my place
in this world

she was just
a wandering soul
trying to find a place
to call home

my soul runs spirited
growing old and rooted
like the doug fir trees
facing the northern wind
strong and steady
i remain centered above the ground
crumbling beneath me

the passion behind
your fragmented sails
will guide you home
this labyrinth is not a place of permanence
but an opportunity to find yourself
and get lost entirely
all over again
there is nothing more profound
than to shed old skin
and become anew
once more

behind every ending
opens another door
to a new beginning

plant your dreams
like you would
a gracious seed
soaking it with
love and light

i relinquish
every forlorn trace
brush off mounds of dust
vanishing
into thin air
these recycled patterns
stem from embedded seeds
of insecurity
of self-deprivation
so i plant them
with love and compassion
and watch them grow
endlessly
from across the land
i will someday blossom in

in order for a flower
to fully bloom
it must learn how to bathe
in both the sunlight
and the rain

the voices in my head
grow quiet about the story
of who it is

i think i have been

and where it is
i am going

i do not need
your permission

to honor my own life

all i need
is to listen to the wind within
when it is calling me home

cleanse
the
body

there is this immense pull
between wanting so badly
to be seen
and wanting so badly
to hide inside the shadows
of my own being

all this running has worn me tired
tired of searching outside myself for peace
consumed with an obsession
over mistrust and cruelty

i throw stones at my body
and then beg for it
to love and nurture me

all the wanting leaves me empty

flashes of sirens emerge
so i sink into my sister's arms
crawling behind couch cushions
crying
screaming
out for his broken arms
but he is deeply buried
inside bottled glass
among strangers
who do not know his name
but only recognize him by
the scars on his hands

is there anybody out there

my body
collapses from its stilt
all that i am now
completely withered
from the crown of my head
down to the corners of my toes
these outcries
they get lost somewhere within
the voice of a distant friend
here i am
my lips
searching for your ears
so you can at once
sink into my uncovered mutters
may you only then find
an understanding of what
i, myself
cannot even begin
to comprehend

tell me
what does it all mean?
to be both
so full
and so empty
at the same time

within all of the chaos
in this world
she just wants to be
understood

sometimes a father
does not know how to feed
the mouths of his children
like the needle he feeds
into his hollow arms

sometimes a mother
does not know how to nurture her young
when she was abandoned by the instinct
that taught her how

sometimes a sister
loses herself in the eyes
of a stranger
who she wished
could fill the empty void
of the father
who did not know how to love
the mother who could not find
the difference between
her connection to multiple dimensions
and her surrounding reality

sometimes a child
whose heart fills with
turmoil and desperation
does not know how to give
nor how to receive
love from those
not defined by chaos
or dysfunction

i'm not quite sure what day of the week it was. or
even what the clock read on the wall. but i sure as hell
knew the fear my eyes witnessed in the empty room.
that is all i knew.

i did not know the lonely series of abandonments i
would carry into adulthood. i did not know i would
relive that loneliness in my head over and over
again. i did not know the comfortable chaos i became
attached to would be imprinted inside my body. the
sirens became louder and more visible from the
living room window. i must have screamed so loud
the neighbors could hear. the door busts open. tears
are shedding. shedding. shedding. strangers wrap me
up in their arms.

i did not know anything at all.

but when i look back on that day
i do know one thing—
all my heart was
begging for. yearning for. crying out for

was just

for someone
for anyone
to stay

christine marie

i often wonder
if the white kitchen ceiling
chipped away from the sounds
of the rumbling hollow pits
inside our caved-in tummies
and hungry-eyed screams

was it the lack of food
or the lack of love
my sisters and i
stood in front of empty cupboards
crying out for

one box left of rice-a-roni

2 a.m. i wake up
push-up after push-up
carving holes inside my skin
just so i wouldn't have to wake up
swollen again
i was once told
not to take up too much space
so instead
i shrank myself small
to the world
i must be human
but i ran out of fuel
after all

i perish in this alchemy
i harden in this dream
spiraling out of control
into invisible steam

dear beautiful body

i apologize for starving you
when you were hungry
and empty

there is this constant pressure
to become better
instead of loving the person
i intrinsically am

in the midst of madness
do you speak gentle words
to yourself
the same way you would
to your Beloved

mirror talk

alone sounds so much more compelling
than convincing a stranger to love
all of the things about myself
i have not yet learned
to love

my chest burns awake at night
shaking away at the thought
of trading its safe space
for the uncertainty of cradling
in the hands of someone
it does not know
maybe this pulsating stone
locked between cracked ribs
cannot bear to settle inside
another broken home

i told him no
he forced himself inside of me
anyway

me too

you treated me like
i was nothing
so nothing
is what i became

sometimes
when i begin
picking apart
my own skin
i find pieces of you
buried inside of me

christine marie

a hidden ocean of grief
wrapped in crushed particles
pours out of my eyes
turning me blind

tucked between my thighs
remnants of your scorpion cells
stick like cemented plaster
between my battered knees

i do not want any other
invading the same womb
you built a home out of

please release me

these foreign hands
lift the blue of you
out of my veins

i have used and have been used

i am sick
of your longing
to have every piece of me

i refuse to belong
to somebody who says
they love me
but cannot ever
tell me
the reasons why

real love
does not look like
your naked body
next to mine

when i am around you
i feel the nothingness
clench between the gaping holes
of my teeth
rotten from biting down
ropes tied to your feet
sacrificing every breath of clean air
my lungs violently breathe

before long
you shove your way
on top of my chest
mangling every limb as they dissembled
from the way your rusty eyes meet
the center of my legs

i am not your property
you cannot take the sea out of me

without drowning your own sails too

what is the point
in welcoming more
into my life
if all i do
is feel empty
inside

i saw you as
my never escaping quicksand
the more i fought
to save myself
the more you
sucked me back in

let me go

you were not afraid
of losing me
you were only afraid
of no longer having
possession over me

christine marie

as she looked into the mirror
he whispered,

black

       and

              blue—

      both

   colors

look

      good

        on you

i confuse the words
i love you
with the bruises
on my back
and the swelling
of my wrists
to be the same

did those bruises
on your knuckles
leave you feeling
whole or
e
      m
          p
             t
                y

spark of internal light
where have you gone
i search inside closet corners
underneath the soles of my feet
these oceanic veins
have now turned into creeks
collecting stones
running slow on crooked teeth

if all your fingers do
is twist at the fibers
i thread myself together with
eventually
there will be nothing left

i carry the shame of his hands
wrapped tightly around my neck
fight so hard to make sweet sweet love
the kind that takes you straight
out of your own body
only to numb the fire that ignites
through his blazing grasp
calloused
frayed
misplaced
i can barely recognize my own face
and so he fills and he fills
the holes of my womanhood
with his power and control
minimizing me
until i am nothing more
than his paper doll

your hands made me feel so small

your poor mother
i think of her often
and how it must feel
to have raised a son
who never learned how to respect
a woman's intelligence
who never learned how to allow
a woman to feed her independence
who never learned how to
kiss a woman's wounds
when she needs stitches
but instead you treat us
like damaged goods
kick us to the curb
when you are bored and finished
you take the sole of your shoe
and press it up against my chest
you have nothing left to give me, you say
you steal your heart out of my hands

you have nothing left

you wanted to build her
a lego house
out of all the pieces
you took from me

nothing stung my heart worse
than seeing her car parked
in the middle of your driveway
where mine used to be

i remember passing her by
sizing her up
as every spark of light
dimmed from her eyes
i wanted to scream

i hope he treats you better
than he did me

but the hollowness of her body
i recognized all too well

it was as if
i was looking at myself in the mirror
one year ago

i thought i was beautiful
i thought i was consumed with love

but what kind of love is worth
losing yourself for

i thought i could hold
the weight of all of you
even the bits and pieces
that didn't make sense to me
but the more of you i held on to
the more pieces of myself
i gave away

you search to find a woman
comfortable in her own skin
yet you stand there intimidated
by my independence

you shrunk me down

a size smaller

just so you could

feel taller

breaking free

is it my fault
will i lose my friends
will they think i am weak
how could i leave
can i forgive him

will they believe me
am i stupid
why did i stay
what if he won't let me
can i forgive myself

i opened up my body to let him in. i allowed him to
grab hold of every single scrap left of me—
relentlessly devouring my insides like i was a piece
of meat he couldn't even bother to savor. licking and
smacking his lips with the same sharp blade he would
use to penetrate my salted wounds. i was afraid of
what would happen if i let him go. so i abandoned
myself instead.

he built me a broken home with his bloody hands. and
i let him in. but i didn't know the strength of his grip.
i didn't know the constant push and pull would exist.
my eyes were swollen and so were my wrists.

but it didn't matter now did it? he had me chewed
up and spit out before i could fight my way out of his
spell. the mirror told me the same stories as him. and
i couldn't escape the shame even if i tried

i couldn't escape the shame even if i tried
i couldn't escape the shame even if i tried

i will never stop trying

i needed you to break me
in order to teach my own body
how to patch itself back together

breaking free

you would have
let me burn
just so i could
keep you warm

i articulate the words
love and hate
to be intertwined
for i have never known
what it is like
to feel one
without the other

i am still searching

i used to
consume myself
with all of your energy
so much that
it replaced my own identity

i never had a home within myself
to come back to

you always made sure of that

i would have stolen parts of you
and molded them into parts of me
that is how much i loved you

i would have become a monster for you

i wanted you to take
all of what i could not bear to carry
on my own
and then
i wanted to blame you
for suffocating underneath
the weight of it all

just so i could find a reason
simply just one reason

to leave you empty-handed
while you turned me
inside out

trauma bond

i am sorry for
when my insecurities
made a monster out of me
i am sorry for
when my jealousy
disrupted the certainty
of the love we shared
i am sorry
for the mess i made
when we were young
and in love

the things i wish you'd say to me

i feel it being pulled out of me—the anguish. the disbelief. the emptiness that once defined every action of my being. every word spit ferociously off my tongue. a loud roar bellows out of me as a foreign language i never imagined i could speak. the weight of the world flies off my shoulders. no longer sticking to a single inch of my skin. i am flying high above the same ground you pushed me on top of. i wipe the dirt off my forehead. i breathe in new air no longer twisted in your scent. i once felt quite low. as low as humanly possible.

not anymore

christine marie

do you know what happens
when the person
who does not love you
releases your hand

you get the chance
to hold your own

you used to be an infection
taking over my system
now you are
barely a symptom

over time
we become calloused
what once made our eyes water
our flames burn out
our bones crumble
indeed
transforms our weaknesses
into inner strengths
we can no longer ignore

but instead of opening up
all that we are made of
we shut down
we stand tall
we phase in and out of others' lives
as a means
to protect ourselves
against the ones who have
phased in and out of
our lives

by shutting down
by blocking the light
from touching our fingertips
the darkness has no way
to disintegrate
we surrender to the places
we swore
we would never
come back to

let the light in

breaking free

like a ghost
you run right through me
haunting me
in the dead of night

i dare not force you away
for this may be the last time i see
the imposed tiny fragments
beneath the mask on your face

so i let you

crawl inside of me

again

i feel

nothing

again

my muscles begin
wasting away
from the absence
of your touch

again

and again

and again

i watch the dust tango
in between worn-down satin
that once soothed me
to sleep
sinking into the outlines
of your hips
naked
i lie here
paralyzed
out of your reach
all i can do now
is picture her shoulder blades
in a casket full of
scattered feathers
where mine used to be

cutting the cord from him freed me of his tie. half of me waits to begin. the other half screams louder. the half that fears losing the only attachment i have left to him. like somehow knowing we are still connected injects equal amounts of bliss and anguish through my bloodstream. that's how it's always been with him though—a twisted paradox of fertilizing a deep intoxicating love and desperately searching for a way out at the very same time.

i never wanted to leave
but i knew i must
if i wanted to
become free

what is the purpose
of love
if it does not start
within

clinging to your love
is like throwing stones
at a house made of glass
shattered
scattered
rays of light illuminate
egocentric spaces
i, the hollowness of this emptiness
grasp for every broken piece
every inch
of your outline
every brush
of artistic lust
every shade
of shadow and white
your mystic oneness
mixed with mine
rosy shades envelope every
unwritten word
into a melancholic poem

but even a song you dance to all night long
does not last
and even a poem stripped down to
every last drop of raw honey
must end

i wish i had known
just how hard it was going to be
to pry my heart space open
once again
after i watched the love we had
fade off into the distance

there is this desire
to give away my love
and give it away
some more
until it completely
dries me empty

what binds us most
is not the disconnection we have
between each other

it is the disconnection
inside the walls
we build
around ourselves

breaking free

just like the wildflowers
in full bloom—

i long to be wild and free

like a tree that loses its leaves
in the dead of winter
i, too, grow tired
of my own permanent nature

as another year passes
holding on to nostalgic branches
reminds me just how temporary
both every ray of sun
and every dark cloud
that vegetates me
is

with my deadened limbs
i spread my arms wide open
for every sprouting root
tangled with the past
as all that has buried me
has planted me a new bed of seeds

and with every changing season
i get another chance
to shed the weight of who i once was
off the layers of my back

Mother Earth
cleanses and replenishes
the soul

let us take gentle care of our Mother
like she has taken gentle care of us

christine marie

the first days of spring
remind me of surviving
the winter storm that once
was you

spinning golden light
radiating--
i am now

letting go of whistling winds
we once woke up listening to
on sunday mornings

our most fatal flaw
is wanting to be loved
by others
without recognizing
the deepest love
mostly comes from
within

don't you see
how courageous it is
to strip apart your pain
and place it in the hands
of infinite strangers

don't you see
how my pain
is yours
and your pain
is mine

so we must
find the strength
to carry it together

most of us spend
entire lifetimes
convincing ourselves
we don't need anybody else
to survive

but we need each other
right here
right now
more than ever
before

it is okay to ask for help

the more beauty
i see
in other women

the more beauty
i see
within myself

i forgive myself
for tolerating
the battered emptiness
you left me with

i forgive myself
because it is
what i thought
i deserved

you almost had me again
but then i remembered
how much you love
turning golden rose petals
into frosted seeds

fall apart at the drop of your name
every bone in my body
kisses the soles of your feet
isn't it ironic
how many times i would
pick
  myself
      apart
just to
      plant
  myself
back
in the very same place
you once had left me

through the foggy mirror
i lend myself a hand
full of compassion
as it is the only hand
i know will save me
in the end

you must learn
how to be
your own best friend

one day you will find out
just how strong you really are
without the weight of past ties

i do not want to be afraid of love
anymore

i wish you could see yourself
the same way others do
your fragile heart
is made of pure gold
you do not know
just how rich
you truly are

you do not owe the world
an explanation
of who it is
you truly are
you only owe it
to yourself
to be true
to yourself

you hold the keys
to all beautiful knowings
in this world

if i keep on paying attention
to my authentic power
the less power my limitations
have over me

lavender bloom dances beneath
a desolate sun
shadows of internal light
share silent nectar
with the buzzing bees
the imperfection of
my physical shape knows
both shallow hope
and deep sorrow
the oneness to all that is pure
roots me down to Mother Earth
in her arms i find nothing more
than tranquil air
that feeds these hollow lungs

here
in her sweet embrace
grace meets me underneath
the bright bellied rays
just as she does
in the pouring rain

innocence sticks like honey
inside shadows
of the wonder wall
as lonely and mystic
as the first morning light
and midnight hour
for who would i be
to embrace one
without the other

the stars remind me
just how small
i really am
a tiny spec of dust
among the shadow
of the trees
oh,
how i'll always strive to be
as big
and as bright
as the moon

i am not as afraid
to fall
as much as i am afraid
to fly

awaken
the
soul

we must learn to love who it is we truly are and never stop seeking until we find our truth.

far too often i have found myself getting lost, stuck inside a labyrinth that has, many times, seemed impossible to pull myself out of. i grew up struggling with many long and dreadful days, sometimes followed by months consumed with extreme episodes of both depression and anxiety—two dark corners most people never talk about or often ignore out of fear of judgment and shame.

these waves of darkness led me into moments of solitude and loneliness that came unwarranted and unexplained. i discovered that the only way to free myself from this vicious cycle was not by wearing a mask or painting myself perfect. instead, it was by finding fulfillment and purpose within my innermost truth. the only way through was by peeling away each and every layer to unearth my very core. true healing begins from the inside out.

by taking the time to connect with myself, the portal to my shadows emerge. my responsibility in these moments is to choose. to choose whether or not to enter into the discomfort of my own humanness.

and so i choose to embark on this path. and i continue to choose facing my afflictions. my grief. my karmic cycles that have guided me to this present state of being. i choose this for the greatest good of self. for the greatest good of all.

with self-compassion and awareness, i welcome in
full presence to my mind. body. and soul. the more
in tune i feel with my whole self, the more i
willingly let go of all things that no longer serve
me. at the end of each day, i fill my body all the way
up with gratitude, for i have carved a path toward a
greater sense of inner peace and alignment than i
have ever known before.

the higher and deeper we are connected to our
mind. body. and soul, the stronger we are in our
abilities to face our fears head on and leap forward
into becoming the spiritual, divine beings we were
born to be.

the only way out of the darkness is through.

this year
i completely unraveled
spitting out my insides
covered in grief
i have now come to befriend
the shame i once released
swallowed whole
by my own shadows
i expose myself out
into the wild
naked and raw
a closed heart space
now shines open
for the world to see
and away my spirit dances
to the music of the trees

christine marie

if i keep holding on to
the trauma seeds
planted inside of me
there will never be room
for anything else
to grow

we may be granted
free will in this life
but do we have enough strength
to save ourselves

i'll find inner peace
once i find inner strength
to speak my truth

we all have an authentic voice
full of fluorescent fire
close your lips
open your ears
and draw in cosmic oxygen
to ignite the flame

christine marie

the core of who we are
cannot be taken from us
without our permission

the lack of
self-compassion
and the art of
self-destruction

are inevitably
the same

soaking in the tears
completely unaware
of how strong self-blame
overcomes good intentions
i take it all personally
i take full responsibility
i wear their sadness on my skin
so they can breathe in
clearer air

self-abandonment

you constantly shamed me
for being too sensitive
when all my heart wanted
was to take the pain
you were too tired to carry
off your hands
and hold it in my own body
when it got too heavy

the irony is
your pain became my own
and as i cried
you shamed me
even more

a vicious cycle

i am a sponge—

soaking in the pain of a stranger
just as i would for someone
i have known all my life

the insides of an empath

the friends who i've lost
the lover whose hand no longer
fits into mine
shatters the soul inside the shell
i deteriorate quietly under
my heart pours down
like a flood of rain
melting into the earth
to feed the hungry flowers
whose strength sprouts
among a season of tears
but i've taken the strong stems
the weak ones, too
and built a home for my heart
to nestle safely into

for the tears i weep
are for the weeping, too

breaking free

i kissed your broken bones
and hugged your emptiness, too

in search of saving you
i lost myself

you cannot fix everything
or everyone
and you can still be loved
and that love
doesn't have to go away

wisdom from my higher self

breaking free

some days
i wish his body to leave this earth
just so his mind could be at peace

christine marie

i just want you to be
proud of me

a daughter's deepest longing

it's easy to forget the light
when we've learned how to grow
in pure darkness

there must be something or someone
keeping me afloat
through the swallowing tides

protection from my spirit guides

if i could whisper to
the little girl
who once was me
i would tell her softly
how her sensitive and vulnerable nature
is what makes her soul
kind and beautiful

i would simply tell her
your empathy
is your greatest gift
for it makes you connected
to all there is

a sense of internal freedom comes alive
once we begin facing our truths
rather than running away
from ourselves

made of love
you are
all that this world needs
more of

a kindred spirit
illuminating all that is
simply
a ray of light
among the shadows
of the darkness

so do not be afraid
to open yourself up
for the light
you give
is just as radiant
as the light within

your wounds are your wisdom

the basic core of who we are
rises
when we surrender to the fear
of falling

unexplainable forces
drag me into fire and ice
squeezing out every drop
until i wring empty
there was nothing left
so i dug and i dug
and i dug some more
running into the dirtiest parts
of me
i've kept underground
for so long
but to uncover our shadows
is to awaken anew
once more

the only way out of the darkness is through

one cannot experience
true joy
without knowing
deep suffering

if you keep on thinking
that loving another will complete you
you will never be whole

two years spent
engraving the outline
of your skeleton
i coursed through every brittle bone
longing   to break
to unwind—   longing
out of revenge

now i lie here
among scattered ashes
collecting dust with the love
we both blindly built up
only to destroy

i met you purely
as a stranger
i remember you
the same

not one
human being
shines quite as bright
as the version of them
you create in your head

if only you knew
all that you are looking for
is what you are already
made of

you are not my universe
i am the center of my own

you helped me see
all of who it is
i truly am

weekly appointments

my body is not a dumping ground
for the cobblestones your shoes collect
while you stumble over the sidewalk cracks
on your karmic path
i am not responsible for the depth of your breath
or the rhythmic beat inside your chest
but i simply cannot leave you lying there
helplessly kissing the ground
for this visceral feeling of empathy
knows how deep your
internal wounds cause
most of your suffering
i know you project parts of yourself
onto my being
my body / your mirror
for your raging fists to crack
i feel sorry for your pain
i feel sorry for your sorrow
but it isn't me who you are angry at
it isn't me
who you want to hurt so bad

this is why embarking on the quest
to love yourself
to come home to your inner knowing
to fall in love with your true being
matters most of all

hurt people hurt people

my therapist says
you can accept and forgive
his heart and soul
but you do not have to
accept and forgive
his behavior

i want to be saved less
and loved more

though we are
worlds apart
my head lay heavy, still
so i begin
rinsing the unforgotten
out of each and every strand
tangled with your scent
watching the midnight shadows
of a past unkind
dance around the drain

the power of moving on
teaches us
how possible it is
to miss the memories
without missing the person
you once shared them with

do not fear
letting go
this—
i've come to know

breaking free

i knew i released you
the moment i stared at the afternoon sun
and did not think of
your golden eyes
anymore

christine marie

you cannot fix
what is meant
to stay broken

our greatest challenges
often become
our greatest teachers

i wonder if
the strength of your love
freed me from
the anchor of him
i was hopelessly
tangled up
and tied to

a sea of grace

the ultimate peace
holds weight in
not being attached
nor defined
by all things
that were never mine
to keep

all of these other men
that hold the same candle
do not melt in your hand
the same way
he once did

darling
please do not
sell yourself short
for who we are
is not determined
by those who love us
or leave us empty

an act of self-love
is allowing those who love you
all the way in
without fear

the bravest thing
we can do
after healing a broken heart
is to take
our bare hands
and break it open
for someone new

the way you look at me
overwhelms the splint inside my chest
beauty
strength
confidence
pouring through me
for the first time
in years

but i am pulling away from you now
this familiar feeling
wraps up my innocence
into a fantasy world

the possibilities of what could be
consume all of me
no matter how high the walls
the fragility of the home that is
my mind / body / soul
is not strong enough
to stand through another love storm
not now
not before
i have spent too much time
building an empire
made up of heartache and loss
only to watch it all crumble
on top of me once again

i have come so far
to build a safety net
around who i am
that i fear welcoming you in
will make me fall farther
than you are willing
to catch me

i wonder
what it feels like
to be loved
effortlessly
by another human being
without expectations
of giving more of yourself
than you are willing

what does it look like
to lie beside
another half-hearted figure
to only realize they are nothing more
than someone who begs to see
far inside your soul
only to come up empty

how can i trust you
when you say you love
all of me
when you do not even know
the half of me

will you stay long enough to learn

christine marie

how can i trust you
when i can't even trust myself

breaking free

my knees buckle
at the thought
of your ear
pressing up against the currents

of my sunken-in chest

maybe this time

you will uncover

the human in me

maybe this time

i will let you

christine marie

the unforgiven past
holds most of its weight
in the present

i thought my mouth was dried up and empty
but then on a wednesday afternoon
the telephone rings
a mutual friend tells me of your old ways
and how you have not changed

i smile

not for the other woman
not for your fixed behavior
but because i am not her
and how beautiful it is
that i once thought to completely change
every ounce of my exterior
to look like her
i was desperate for you to want me
the way you wanted her
and now i wish to never be
anywhere close to becoming her
i want nothing to do
with you wanting any part of me

i only want you to someday
open your eyes
and begin to see
how your lips taste like poison
how your hands melt like lava
how you dissolve fresh flesh
just so you could fall asleep
every night without hunger
while we starve to death

i weep

i hope one day she finds the strength
to set herself free

forgiving someone
looks like trying on their shoes
and fully accepting
that their impersonal actions or words
stem from a pain so deep
you, yourself
cannot visibly see
with the naked eye

while the words
i love you
mean forever
to most

to us
they mean
letting go

i remember wishing that it would end. the ache. the agony. the grief that once made my head spin and my heart sink at even the slightest drop of your name. but after the constant twist came the pause. what was birthed anew was the missing. the missing of the melancholy of it all just to feel alive and human again. but i could not dare let myself give in to the familiar nightfall of affliction.

a new day unearthed as i awoke in a haze. dreaming of you now is so much different than it has ever been. i no longer claw at the sheets for the nightmare to vanish. no longer sink myself into a deeper sleep in hopes of seeing the details of the corners where your lips meet your cheeks. no longer replay the sound of the voice that once made my eyes water. no longer carry the weight of your shadows while my shoulders disintegrate into a million little pieces.

you are now an old, rusted notebook falling apart at the seams. begging to be thrown away on its last ends while never forgetting the lessons stained in permanent ink. the loss of you no longer brings me to my knees.

you are now another part of ancient history.

red flags wave
the curtain of night closes in
all at once
loneliness appears
i bear witness
to it all
when he told me
he did not deserve me
i knew he was not going to let himself
love me anymore
than the best of his ability
i, in return
mirrored that capacity
there is no wonder
why we did not make it through
i shed hope that someday
we both awaken separately
and begin giving ourselves the kind of love
we deserve

breaking free

true healing lies
behind the eyes of those
who recognize beauty
in both the darkness
and the light

the awareness to
your observing mind
is the jewel
to your awakening

breaking free

everything i once believed in

no longer carries me

i would rather surrender
surrender all of the
sheltered limbs
of my dignity
than to live a life
full of bitter ignorance
clouded by a veil of illusion

raising consciousness

breaking free

i lose sleep over
my dreams
tireless fantasies
passing me by
but isn't this breath
this act of living
of being alive

a dream in itself

one must not confuse production
with lack of consciousness
when you create from your inner space
without pressure
without expectations
without resistance
the flow of spirit rushes in
and spits out
every unspoken beacon
of ancient wisdom

your inner
and outer worlds
have been waiting
lifetimes upon lifetimes upon lifetimes
to merge

trust the process

what if every day
we choose to wake up
with the belief
that who we are
is more than
good enough
imagine
just imagine—
if we were often this brave
this connected
this compassionate
right here
and right now
who it is
we could become

answer spirits call

once you begin to embrace your vulnerabilities
and open yourself up to the world
the world responds with more love
more compassion
more truth
than you could possibly imagine

the only person holding you back from your
destiny
is the person staring back at you
in the mirror

let go of your fear of failure
and trust your ethereal interior
to guide you back home

disconnection is a violent illness
and we are all suffering
now more than ever before

we connect
through our vulnerabilities
and oh,
how uncovering our truth
swarms our spines
bringing us closer
to internal peace

by reaching out
toward one another
by combining
our innermost
fears and uncertainty
it inevitably
pulls us toward
a deeper understanding
within ourselves

that is indeed
the ultimate
human gratification

that is indeed
the dose of medicine
needed to heal the collective

there is a reason
we survive off compassion
and human connection
if you and i are one
there is no wonder
why i find pieces of myself
buried in the eyes
of your soul

my soul is here
to create a template
from scars that bind
with the infinite
so i raise my vibrations
welcoming in the
sweetest sound of divinity
to unleash my destiny
to gather thy medicine
for my brothers and sisters
to heal their soul bodies

if i must continue
to transform
i must let go
the feeling
of control

how imperative
it is
to accept the many dark
lonely avenues
i must take
to find the way
back home to my higher self
back home to my little girl

surrender to what is true
there is no law when it comes to
following your intuition

breaking free

so i walk with my eyes closed
until the outside static
quietly dissipates
and i can hear the sound
of my native heart
the sound
of my sacred breath
the rooting firmness of the soles
wrestling through
the stones of Mother Earth
my compass into
the vast spaciousness
of all that is connected
of all that exists
of all that there is
of all that i am

the path to awakening is not about seeing
it is about trusting
i am exactly
where i am supposed to be

i must keep going
i must sacrifice all of who it is
i've convinced myself i am
so i can truly become
what this world needs more of

healing

it was not so much about leaving you
more than it was about
finding who i was
who i could be
who i was meant to be
without your gust of wind
weighing down my wings
plucking apart my feathers
from the very same back
you pinned against brick walls
and basement floors

it was only when i surrendered
to the army of colors
both around and inside of me
when these rusted eyes began to notice
how bright the ethereal sun
shines through the black and blue pores
your fingertips once painted over

and it is only when
i found beauty in the way
the colors of my spine
harmonized along
the colors in the sky
that my spirit soared higher
than it ever did
bound by the person
who held down these wings

i am finally free

by giving myself full permission to open up. to
become a different kind of vulnerable. to dive into
the depths of both my shadow and my light,
acceptance of self has become a daily practice. the
fear of selfishness dissolves as i realize i am unable
to heal. inspire. or create profound change if i do not
take the time and space to nurture and strengthen
the bones that keep me emotionally safe and
grounded.

the awakening has begun to emerge—cultivating a
deeper connection to self and to spirit than i ever
thought possible. the less identification i give to my
past traumas, the less power they have over me. all of
the pain and suffering is only a part of my story. it is
not who i am.

when i was buried inside the dark night of the soul,
my connection to spirit and the birth of my true
divinity was what held me through the sleepless
nights and lonely days.

i uncovered the power of stillness. of presence. of
surrender. of oneness. and by doing so, i interlaced
each and every finger with my higher self and she
became my guiding light. i look ahead toward the rest
of my awakening journey with a smile and a sense of
peace in knowing that this is just the beginning.

the seeker in me—the sensitive empath who longs
to find a place in this physical world—will forever
seek refuge back home to her little girl. the
unavoidable burning spark in the center of my
chest is the north star that will forever light my
way through the darkness. as i follow the path to
my destiny, that flame of hope will never die
within me.

i am proud of the progress i have made thus far
and am filled with immense gratitude for all i have
learned and will continue to learn in this lifetime. i
will do my best to allow my heart space to remain
open with fierce love and compassion and to protect
my energy in times of need.

i give myself permission on my spiritual adventure
to fall. to rise. to rest. and to be alive in the present
moment without worries of past ties or future
reservations.

i thank myself for being brave and vulnerable
on the days i feel small and afraid.

Mother India is calling
and i must go

with lovingkindess,

christine marie

my deepest gratitude

to my spirit family for the bountiful
protection and unconditional love.

to my higher self who chose this lifetime to be born
into the traumas. the challenges. and the many
lessons i was meant to learn. for if it wasn't for those
shades of darkness, i would not have unearthed the
wisdom and medicine to heal myself and others.

to my mother and father for birthing me into this
world. for trying your best. and for highlighting my
souls purpose through the various lessons your
stories teach me every day.

to the army of soul sisters who have stuck by my side.
who have held my hand as i grieved. who have
celebrated my joy and my wins. who have been there
through thick and thin. i love you unconditionally.

to my aunt and uncle who sacrificed their lives to
raise me and my sisters. who fought relentlessly to
carve a better path for us. who put a roof over our
heads when we didn't have one. who fed us food when
our bellies were empty. who embraced us when no
one else was willing. i thank you for your love.

to my entire blood family for the support and love
you've generously given so whole-heartedly to me.
to my olders sisters deidre and melissa. to my
childhood soul sisters victoria and shannon. all who
have witnessed my journey since a young girl. who
held me close and have carved out a path for me
greater than i could have ever known.

to my loving coaches and dear friends victoria
morris, jordan aftanas, and shannon kaiser. if it
wasn't for your ongoing support. encouragement.
and guiding lights—this dream would not have
come to fruition. thank you for your knowledge.
your wisdom. and your belief in
this medicine.

to my therapist who fully sees me. who allows me
to express my truth fully. your support and space
holding changed my life.

to mother earth. to the sacred lands of every place
i've lived and traveled. thank you for your warm
embrace. sustenance. and spaciousness.

and to you, the reader. for being brave and willing
enough to read these words. to take the time and
space to nourish and love yourself. the world needs
you and your light. do not let another day go by
without shining it.

about the author

at nine years old, christine was hospitalized with
a rare lung disease that almost took her life. it was
during this life event when she realized she could not
leave this lifetime without fully living her purpose.
her soul yearned to fulfill three dreams—to become
a nurse. to travel the world. and to write a book about
her life story.

at 23 years old, she had already journeyed to
several countries. graduated with a nursing degree.
and moved across the country by herself from
michigan to oregon. she didn't know it then, but
her move to the pacific northwest led her to
discover herself in ways she had neglected.

while meeting the dark night, she found a deep sense
of comfort in the hands of her higher self and spirit.
it was then when her heart remembered she had one
dream left to grant her little girl—birthing her first
book, *breaking free*.

christine marie

a poet. mystic. traveling free spirit.
nurse. photographer. energy healer.
cosmic creator—

christine marie is an intuitive empath and
gatherer of divine medicine to heal herself
and the collective.

her creative self-expression is used as a portal back
to her true self and her inner knowing.
an advocate for positive change
around de-stigmatizing
mental health
domestic violence and
human disconnection—

she urges the need for more self-love.
self-reflection. and spiritual connection. in order
to create a more conscious, loving
human evolution.

Made in the USA
Middletown, DE
03 June 2021

40971170R00149